Fashion **through the Ages**

Uniforms

Copyright © ticktock Entertainment Ltd 2006
First published in Great Britain in 2006 by ticktock Media Ltd.,
Unit 2, Orchard Business Centre, North Farm Road,
Tunbridge Wells, Kent, TN2 3XF
ISBN 1 86007 982 2
Printed in China
A CIP catalogue record for this book is available from the British Library.

Picture credits
t=top, b=bottom, c=centre, l-left, r=right

Bridgeman Art Library: 6-7c, 7 all, 13 all, 18 all, 23b. Corbis: 16-17c, 17t. South American Pictures: 20-21 all. Werner Forman: 8-9
all, 10-11 all.

Every effort has been made to trace the copyright holders, and we apologise in advance for any unintentional omissions.
We would be pleased to insert the appropriate acknowledgements in any subsequent edition of this publication.

CONTENTS

• *Glossary terms are boldened on first use on each spread*

3

INTRODUCTION

Originally, the word 'uniform' was just a way of describing things that all looked or felt the same. But today, 'uniform' is mostly used as the name for a type of clothing. It must be made in a specific colour or design and worn by many people, for the same purpose.

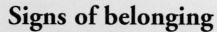

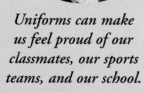

Uniforms can make us feel proud of our classmates, our sports teams, and our school.

When was the Red Cross organisation founded?

In 1863 by Swiss philanthropist Henri Dunant.

Signs of belonging

Some uniforms are cheap and simple, others are costly and elaborate. They may be home-made, purchased from shops, or given to wearers by the people they work for. Each different uniform shows that the wearer belongs to one special group – a school, an army, a profession or a band – or a thousand other organisations. Uniforms also help people feel that they belong together.

A sense of tradition

Many uniforms feature traditional garments or symbolic colours. They may date from a time when the group that first wore them achieved great success or won famous victories. Uniforms can also symbolise past values – such as courage and team spirit – that leaders wish to encourage today. They can stand for political ideas or political beliefs that organisations wish to protect or preserve.

Evzones (guards) on duty in Greece. They are wearing a dress uniform (for special occasions), based on tunics and jackets worn by famous Greek freedom-fighters 500 years ago.

The familiar white coat of a vet or doctor instantly identifies the wearer as a medical professional, and offers reassurance to the patient.

Great expectations

Uniforms change the way we behave – because they represent the qualities we expect to find in the people who wear them. We usually trust uniformed nurses, and expect them to be kind. But we fight against – or flee from - soldiers wearing enemy kit. Sometimes rebels usually choose to wear some uniform items. These identify them to their enemies – but also to their comrades, so that they do not accidentally attack each other in battle.

Professional pride

Many uniforms are linked to professions and occupations. They are designed to be practical and, if need be, protective, such as the tough overalls worn by engineering workers, or the waterproof jackets and trousers worn by police motorcyclists. Uniforms also help create a favourable image of each profession. Orchestral musicians wear discreet but glamorous evening dress. Executives from multinational companies all choose smart, sober, tailored suits, to show that they are serious about the work they do.

A symphony orchestra dressed in typical uniform - evening dresses for women and suits and shirts for the men.

THE FIRST UNIFORMS

The first official uniforms were made around 2,000 years ago. But people were putting on clothes, jewels and make-up to display their identity and group membership many centuries earlier.

Maori men and women from New Zealand perform a traditional dance.

Dancing together

Few examples of prehistoric uniforms have survived until today. But ancient styles are preserved by people who still practise traditional arts, such as dancing.

Their clothes reflect the origins of their dances, such as coming-of-age rituals. In war-dances, warriors wore body paint to display their rank and bravery. In religious rituals, dancers all dressed in the same way to confuse evil spirits who might be waiting to attack.

Ghost Dancers

Some uniforms were believed to have magical powers. They might be made of special materials such as certain animal skins, or be decorated with **talismans** (objects with alleged magical powers). Belief in these uniforms continued for thousands of years. In the 19th century, for example, Native Americans fighting against European settlers joined a religious movement known as the Ghost Dance Society. Members wore special shirts, said to have supernatural powers.

Ghost Dance shirt, made of fringed deerskin and decorated with birds and stars.

Larger than life

Many traditional uniforms were designed to terrify enemies by making the men who wore them seem larger than life. Feather 'war-bonnets', worn in many parts of North and South America, increased the wearer's height by up to half a metre. In southern Africa, Zulu soldiers wore head-dresses made from lions' manes. As well as increasing height, this headgear also suggested that Zulu men shared the power and strength of 'the king of the beasts'.

This Zulu warrior from South Africa was photographed around 1890.

What happened to the Ghost Dancers?

Most of them were killed in battle. Their magic shirts were no protection against bullets.

Healers set apart

In many past societies, **shamans** (magic healers) believed they could get help from the gods by drumming, fasting, or taking potions made of fungi and herbs. For these healing rituals, shamans put on special clothes or disguised themselves with masks. This 'uniform' set them apart from ordinary people and allowed them to behave in unusual ways. Today, the white uniforms worn by doctors send out a similar message. They suggest that doctors are special people, who act in a trained, professional manner. They make it acceptable for doctors to do things, such as examine patients, that ordinary people would not be allowed to do.

A Blackfoot shamen (magic healer) from North America

7

ANCIENT EGYPT AND ITS NEIGHBOURS

The hot, dry climate of North Africa meant that most Ancient Egyptians wore very few clothes. In spite of this, the differences between their garments were extremely important. Each item of Egyptian clothing, headgear and jewellery displayed its wearer's wealth, rank or occupation.

A wall painting of an Egyptian Pharaoh carrying a crook and flail, and dressed in a striped headdress.

Royal symbols

The Egyptians believed that their Pharaohs (kings) were not just ordinary rulers. They were superhuman. As a sign of their god-like powers, pharaohs wore crowns, or a special striped **nemes** headdress, and carried a **crook** (hooked stick) and a **flail** (a heavy rod). The crook was used by shepherds to rescue sheep; it was a sign of the Pharaoh's care for his people. The flail was used for threshing grain; it represented strength and fertility.

Pure and holy

Pharaohs and their senior wives had many religious duties. They shared these with priests and priestesses, recruited from noble Egyptian families. Before taking part in religious rituals, priests and priestesses had to be pure. They washed all over, and shaved all the hair from their heads and bodies. They dressed in clean white kilts or tunics, woven from linen. Wool and leather were thought to be unclean. The only animal products permitted were beautiful, valuable leopard-skins, worn by 'sem' (high-ranking) priests and priestesses.

A senior priestess, draped in leopard-skin, sits in front of a table laden with offerings for the gods.

For valour

Egypt was defended on all sides by natural barriers – deserts, **cataracts** (waterfalls on the River Nile) and the sea. Yet all able-bodied Egyptian men still had a duty to serve in the Pharaoh's army. They wore their own clothes and supplied their own weapons, but, if they fought well, they might be rewarded by the Pharaoh with eye-catching medals. Shaped liked flies, these medals told onlookers that the wearer had bravely 'stung' the enemy, and deserved honour.

These fly-shaped medals, awarded for valour, are made of real gold.

Why were Egyptian medals shaped like flies?

Probably because being stung by real Egyptian flying insects could be serious.

Battle technology

In lands close to Egypt, Mesopotamian peoples were famous for pioneering new ways of fighting. By around 2500 BC, they had invented the first-known padded metal helmets, and the earliest armoured clothing. To begin with, soldiers wore leather cloaks, covered with domed discs of hammered metal. Later, the discs were replaced by overlapping metal plates, sewn on to tunics made of leather. After around 1500 BC, Assyrians also began to wear hob-nailed boots for fighting, rather than open-toed sandals. All these garments gave Mesopotamian soldiers an advantage over their enemies. They also acted like a national uniform, making them instantly recognisable.

Assyrian relief carving, dating from between 880-612 BC

ANCIENT GREECE AND ITS NEIGHBOURS

Ancient Greece was divided into hundreds of city-states. So there was no single style of dress, but Greek city-states were all loyal to their own ancient customs and traditions. These formed the basis of distinctive local 'uniforms', in clothing, weapons and armour.

In the city-state of Sparta, slave soldiers always wore red tunics.

What uniforms did the ancient Greeks wear to compete in the Olympics?

Athletes ran wearing nothing at all!

Written symbols

Each Greek city-state was defended by an army of '**hoplites**' (foot-soldiers) and **cavalry**. Men from the same state all wore similar armour, made in local styles. For example, in Sparta, officers' helmets usually had a crest running sideways over the head, from ear to ear. Elsewhere, Greek helmets had crests running from front to back.

Foreign helpers

Rich and powerful city states, such as Athens, employed troops from neighbouring countries to help protect their community. They recruited archers from Scythia (lands bordering the Black Sea) to fight in their armies and serve as a city police force. Scythians wore their own local costume, which became their 'uniform'. It included trousers, a tunic, and a close-fitting cap.

A Scythian archer, portrayed in an Athenian vase-painting. He is wearing typical Scythian clothes, and carries a quiver, for arrows, slung from a belt around his waist.

Role-play

The Greeks invented **drama** – plays that acted out religious myths or described the adventures of famous local heroes. performing in a drama, or watching in the audience, was a religious act . Everyone in the theatre was honouring the gods. To play their parts, actors put on wigs, masks and padded costumes. By dressing in this 'uniform', actors hid their real faces, but showed very clearly the thoughts or feelings of the characters they portrayed.

This vase painting shows actors in masks, playing an old man (left) who is helping a handsome young lover (right) climb up to the window of his lady love.

Persian pride

Greek city states also joined together also joined to fight against foreign invaders, such as the mighty Persian army that invaded in the 5th century BC. The Persians ruled a vast empire, and recruited soldiers from any different local tribes. Some wore tunics and trousers similar to the Scythians. Others dressed in shirts and short, wrapped skirts (rather like kilts). All these local clothes served as a 'uniform', helping soldiers to recognise comrades, and inspiring feelings of local loyalty and pride.

Figurine of a warrior, c.490 BC (bronze)

11

THE ANCIENT ROMAN EMPIRE

Uniforms are often a sign of a strong, central government that has the power to decide upon standard styles of clothing. Between around 100 BC and 400 AD, the Ancient Romans ruled the mightiest empire the world had yet seen. Roman troops were some of the first to wear a simple kind of uniform.

Army issue

The earliest Roman soldiers were all Romans citizens. At first, they wore their own, local clothes. Later, these were provided by army officers, based on standard (or 'uniform') designs. As a sign of rank, Roman officers wore red cloaks and had horsehair crests in their helmets. After around 100 BC, the Roman empire grew rapidly, and the Romans began to recruit soldiers from conquered lands. Each legion wore its own local clothes, such as Celtic trousers, or tight-fitting caps from Gaul (now France).

A Roman officer around AD 150. He wears a typical Roman tunic, helmet and armour, plus short trousers copied from auxiliary soldier styles.

For fighting and dying

In the first and second centuries AD, deadly fights between gladiators were very popular in Rome. Fighters dressed in different uniforms. A **secutor** had tough leather armour on his left leg, wrists and elbows. A **murmillo** wore a heavy helmet and carried a long square shield. A retiarius had just one shoulder covered, but was armed with a net and **trident** (three pronged spear). Usually, a heavily armoured man fought against a less well protected one.

A Roman gladiator, wearing a shoulder protector.

Toga wearing politicians in an illustration of the Roman senate.

Why were Roman army tunics red?

Roman soldiers may have been copying their officers. Or they may have worn red because it hid blood and helped stop wounded men panicking in battle.

White, bright or purple?

For peaceful activities, a toga was the usual clothing worn by Roman men. It was a large semi-circular cloak, made of natural beige or white wool, draped round the body in complicated folds. Foreigners and slaves were not allowed to wear them. There were different types of toga. High-ranking **senators** (members of Rome's governing council) wore togas with a deep purple border. Emperors' togas were purple all over. Politicians running for office had their togas washed in a special clay-type mixture. This gave their clothes a bright finish. They became known as '**candidates**' (Latin for 'white-robed') – a word we still used today.

Covering up

Roman men and women always covered their heads when making offerings to their household's guardians spirits. They used a fold of their tunic, or a loose corner of their cloak, to turn their everyday dress into a religious 'uniform'. But priests and priestesses wore a extra veil, called a suffibulum. It symbolised holiness, purity and **piety** (respect for the gods), and was draped over the back of the head, covering the neck and shoulders. Images of women wearing this veil were often used on Roman coins, to encourage Roman citizens to follow traditional rules for good behaviour.

A Vestal Virgin priestess wearing an elaborate head-band, plus a suffibulum veil over her shoulders.

MEDIEVAL EUROPE

In early medieval Europe, there were no official uniforms. But between AD 1000 and AD 1500, changes in the Christian Church, and also new ways of fighting, led to the development of many specially-designed clothes.

Fighting mad

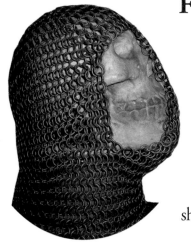

Chain mail was suopposed to protect the wearer from sword blows, but was very cumbersome.

Armies were some of first places where real uniforms developed. Among the Vikings of Scandinavia, specially savage warriors wore tunics made of bear-skin. Known as **Berserkers** (bear-shirts), they worked themselves up into a fury, shouting, stamping and chewing their shields. New technology also led to warriors wearing the same kinds of clothes. In the early medieval era, most warriors wore **chain-mail**. But this was replaced by new **plate armour** (personal armour made from large metal plates, worn on the chest and sometimes the entire body).

What uniform did medieval Christians wear to show they were sorry for their sins?

Coarse, rough, scratchy sack-cloth (because it made them suffer) plus a sprinkling of ashes (to symbolise death and decay).

Heraldry

It was difficult for soldiers wearing armour to look from side to side, or to turn round quickly. So, to help recognise friends - and foes – in battle, medieval fighting men painted patterns on their shields and surcoats (loose cloth robes, worn on top of armour). Each noble family had its own design, which was also worn by its followers, like a uniform. Royal servants learned all the different designs, and organised them into a new picture language, called 'heraldry'.

This 15th century painting features the heraldic shields of the von Esendorf family.

Holy habits

The Christian Church was the most powerful organisation in medieval Europe. Its influence spread throughout the continent, ignoring national boundaries. It encouraged believers to live apart from the world, in communities of monks and nuns. To show that they were holy, and dedicated to God, monks and nuns wore dark, drab uniforms called '**habits**'. Ordinary priests and Church leaders also wore long dark garments. But they added magnificent coloured vestments (holy robes) to take part in church services. These included mitres (hats), stoles (scarves) and copes (cloaks).

One of the Göss Vestments, made in the 13th century for priests. The vestment featured squares with birds and mythical beasts beautifully embroidered upon it.

Professional costume

Most medieval men and women were peasant farmers, who made a living from farming. Their clothes were plain and simple, and usually home-made. But, towards the end of the medieval era, new groups of professional people began to work in Europe. These ranged from doctors, lawyers and professors to singers, dancers and jesters (clowns). Most had their own special uniform. Learned men wore dark robes similar to monk's habits. But entertainers wore amazing costumes in bright, contrasting colours.

A 14th century medieval illustration of a doctor about to perform an eye operation.

15

Asia is home to many different civilisations, with different customs and traditions. Most have uniforms for military or ceremonial wear. Some are worn only locally, others are worn over a wide area. Everywhere they are influenced by local political, economic and environmental conditions.

Religious robes

Buddhism was founded by an Indian prince called Gautama Siddhartha. After meditating (thinking deeply), he came to believe that humans could only find happiness by giving up earthly passions, such as greed and envy. Followers called him Buddha, which means 'the enlightened one'. To symbolise their devotion to Buddha's ideas, young men shave their heads and wear a simple **saffron**-coloured (orange) robes to show they are monks.

A Buddhist monk in Thailand.

Guarding the emperor

Chinese warrior prince Zheng was the first ruler to unite the separate, warring states of China. He founded the first Chinese empire, and took a new title Qin Shi Huangdi (all-powerful Chinese emperor). He recruited a new army, introduced new laws, coins, weights and measures, and employed a new civil services. When Qin Shi Huangdi died, his body was buried in a magnificent tomb. Thousands of lifelike **terracotta** (baked clay) warriors were buried close by, to guard his spirit. These clay figures show us what their uniforms looked like.

Each terracotta warrior is dressed in uniform: there are several different styles.

Muslim Sufi dancers, called dervishes, wore long caftans originating in Central Asia) and tall domed hats.

Whirling dervishes

The faith of Islam was founded by the Prophet Muhammad, who died in Arabia in AD 632. Muslims all shared the same basic beliefs, but they could not all agree to follow the same leaders. The majority, Sunni, group were led by **caliphs** (rulers chosen by believers), and guided by the Sunna (example) set by Muhammad during his life. The minority, known as Shia, preferred leaders descended from the Prophet Muhammad's close family. The Shia also tolerated different ways of worshipping, including **sufi** mysticism which practiced meditation to try to reach god, and holy 'dervish' dancing.

Who else was buried with emperor Qin Shi Huangdi?

The workers who designed and built his tomb, and who laid his body to rest there.

Entertainment industry

Throughout Asia, women – and some men – worked hard to keep onlookers happy. Some were actors, musicians or temple dancers. In Japan, a specially chosen few were trained as geisha (elegant entertainers). For all these tasks, performers put on distinctive clothes that were often just like a uniform. They often also took part in religious or political rituals. Some were princesses, decked with jewels.

Two modern geishas dressed in the distinctive costumes and white makeup.

17

AFRICA

Africa is a vast continent, with many different languages and traditions. In the past, formal uniforms were rare. But top soldiers often wore similar clothing to their comrades, and ordinary soldiers throughout Africa relied on traditional beliefs, rather than specialised clothes, for protection.

The 'Honor of Trousers'

The kingdom of Mali, in northern West Africa, controlled a wide empire. Mali's greatest ruler was King Mansa Musa (reigned 1312-1337). His troops fought on horseback and on foot. **Cavalrymen** dressed in metal helmets, spiked collars and breastplates, plus cotton robes. To reward brave, successful soldiers, Mali rulers created the 'Honour of the Trousers', handing over splendid garments for each courageous deed or victory. The soldiers who wore the largest number of trousers, all at once, could easily be recognised as the bravest and the best.

A modern illustration of King Mansa Musa, King of Mali.

These warriors belonged to the Leopard Hunters Guild.

Animal power

The kingdom of Benin (now part of Nigeria, West Africa), was powerful from around 1400-1700. Its top warriors belonged to a secret brotherhood called the Leopard Hunters' Guild. In battle, they wore uniform helmets and armour made from a most unusual material - tough, scaly anteater skin. Anteaters were one of the few creatures that could survive being attacked by leopards. By wearing anteater skins, Benin warriors got practical protection from sharp leopard teeth and claws.

Magical protection

Ordinary soldiers throughout Africa could not afford fine uniforms made from valuable animal skins. So they went into battle naked or dressed in everyday clothes. These ranged from wrapped cloth garments to brief leather aprons or simple tunics woven from tough fibrous plants.

In central Africa, for example, warriors in Kongo (now Zaire), made uniforms out of palm leaves. Instead of uniforms and armour many African soldiers trusted to fetishes (magic amulets) for safety, and used bells and rattles to summon helpful spirits or drive evil ghosts away.

An African fetish from the Democratic Republic of Congo, Africa.

Islamic Influences

The faith of Islam reached North Africa between AD 700-800. It spread slowly to other parts of the continent, carried by soldiers and traders. In many parts of Africa, colours had important symbolic meanings. West African Muslims, in particular, believed that white was the colour of joy. They wore white clothes on Fridays, the Muslim holy day, when believers rest from work and go to mosques to listen to preachers and pray alongside fellow members of their community.

What uniform was given to dead people?

Plain white hand-woven cloth. This tradition may have had links with Ancient Egyptian customs.

A 19th century photograph of a Muslim from Ghana dressed in traditional uniform.

19

THE AMERICAS

The many different peoples living in North and South America each wore their own local kinds of clothes. But, however different these garments looked like, they were usually made from local materials, and included signs and symbols identifying wealth, rank and beliefs.

An Aztec Eagle Knight, dressed for battle.

Strict control

Among the Aztecs of Meso-America, the right to wear different styles of clothing was strictly controlled. Unmarried girls left their hair loose; married women wore braids with the ends pointing upwards like horns. Only noblemen were allowed to wear cloaks reaching below the knee. The best, most courageous, soldiers, known as 'Eagle Knights' and 'Jaguar Knights' wore magnificent uniforms fashioned from real feathers and wild animal skins.

Signs of distinction

In North America, high-ranking chiefs, warriors and shamans (magic healers) wore clothes that displayed their high status. For practical reasons, these people wore the same basic clothing as ordinary men and women – typically a robe or tunic and trousers of deerskin (common among northern Native nations), or patterned woven blankets and wraps (usual among western desert peoples). These simple garments had splendid trimmings of fur, feather, beaks, shells, teeth and bones.

For religious rituals, important people put on animal disguises, body-paint and masks.

Puritan men who settled in America wore wool or linen shirts, together with fitted jackets and knee-breeches.

Religious symbols

Many of the first Europeans to settle in North America migrated there for religious reasons. They wanted freedom to live and worship in the way they thought best. From the 1620s onwards, their clothes were based on styles worn by other 'Puritans' (religious reformers) in Europe. They favoured plain, simple, modest clothing, in dark colours, without fancy trimmings, such as frills, lace or embroidery. Over time, clothing evolved to suit America's harsh climate. These included hard-wearing **buckskin** boots and jerkins (close-fitting, hip-length, collarless jacket), and fur lined hats and cloaks for warmth.

Who else, apart from Aztec nobles, was allowed to wear long cloaks?

Ordinary soldiers whose legs had been badly scarred in battle.

Conquistadors

In the late 17th and 18th centuries, rival Europeans battled for control of the Americas. In Mexico, Spanish forces led by Hernan Cortes landed in central Mexico in 1519. They fought and conquered the native Aztec people in the space of just two years. While the native Aztecs dressed in clothing designed for symbolic importance rather than to aid them in battle, the Spanish conquistadors were clad in iron for protection in battle. In Peru, Spanish forces dressed in metal armour and led by Francisco Pizarro quickly overcame the cloth-clad Inca forces.

Spanish forces clad in iron armour battle against Aztec forces in Mexico.

EUROPE 1500 ~ 1750

By around 1500, kings, popes and other important people in Europe were beginning to issue their servants with uniforms, rather than simple **surcoats** or heraldic badges. Certain colours - especially red and black - were increasingly linked with particular professions.

Swiss Guards and Beefeaters

Since Roman times, European rulers had recruited troops of elite soldiers to guard themselves, their palaces and their families. By around 1500, many royal bodyguards were wearing specially-designed uniforms. In Italy, the Swiss Guards, who protected the Pope, wore striped tunics and breeches of red and gold. In England, the Yeoman of the Guard (founded in 1485 to protect King Henry VII at his coronation), also wore red uniforms, with a gold cipher (heraldic pattern) on the front of their tunics representing the ruling monarch's initials.

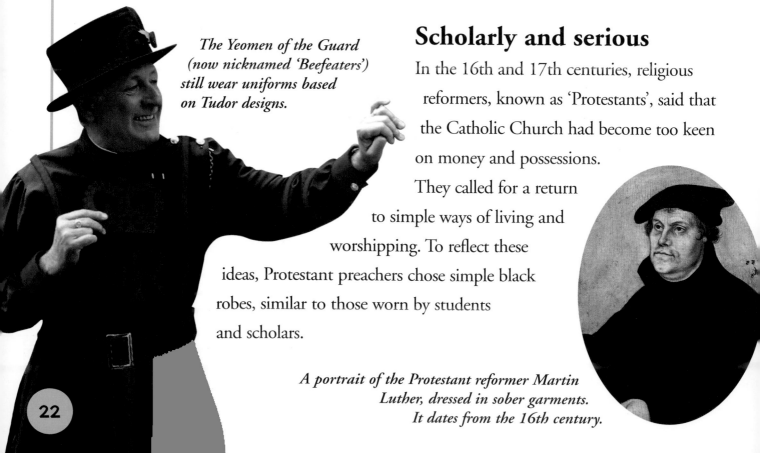

The Yeomen of the Guard (now nicknamed 'Beefeaters') still wear uniforms based on Tudor designs.

Scholarly and serious

In the 16th and 17th centuries, religious reformers, known as 'Protestants', said that the Catholic Church had become too keen on money and possessions. They called for a return to simple ways of living and worshipping. To reflect these ideas, Protestant preachers chose simple black robes, similar to those worn by students and scholars.

A portrait of the Protestant reformer Martin Luther, dressed in sober garments. It dates from the 16th century.

Masked party-goers dance in the streets to the exciting beat of a carnival drum (played by musician, far right).

In disguise

Catholic countries in southern Europe continued to celebrate traditional Church festivals with special entertainments. To mark the start of Lent - 40 solemn days of fasting and **repentance** (being sorry for sins) before Easter - they held feasts and parties, called carnivals. At carnival time, merry-makers wore uniforms that included masks and fancy dress, so that no-one could tell who they were or criticise them for bad behaviour. Carnival masks became a kind of unofficial uniform. It was almost unthinkable to attend a carnival party without one.

Goodbye to meat'. Believers were meant to give up meat and other favourite foods during Lent.

What does the word 'carnival' mean?

National identity

After around 1700, most professional soldiers had some kind of official uniform. But volunteers continued to wear their own clothing for war. They displayed loyalty to comrades and commanders by wearing coloured scarves or bunches of tough local plants, such as oak-leaves, pinned to their clothing. Local clothing was also chosen by rebels as a symbol of defiance against the ruling country. In Scotland, for example, Jacobite rebels fought against the Hanoverian dynasty (who ruled Britain 1714-1837). Ordinary Jacobite soldiers wore their local dress - a kilt and plaid (length of fabric draped like a cloak). So did the Scottish nobles who led them.

Portrait of William Cumming, Piper to the Laird of Grant, 1714

23

The late 18th and 19th centuries are often called a 'golden age' of army and navy uniforms. For officers, and many ordinary enlisted men, uniform clothes were more elaborate, colourful and varied than ever before.

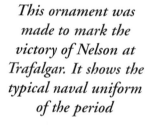

This ornament was made to mark the victory of Nelson at Trafalgar. It shows the typical naval uniform of the period

Naval discipline

Naval uniforms clearly displayed the wearer's rank. In Britain, for example, crewmen wore natural beige woollen or linen shirts, with wide 'bell-bottom' trousers; officers wore navy-blue blue jackets with tight white knee-breeches (trousers extending down to or just below the knee). Senior officers' jackets were decorated with **epaulettes** (a fringed strap worn on military uniforms), gold braid plus badges won for bravery. Crewmen were usually bare-headed; officers wore tall hats, with **rosettes** (badges made of ribbon or silk) or bunches of feathers.

Thin red line

Uniforms worn by soldiers were based on late 18th century fashions - tight knee-breeches (later replaced by long tight trousers), plus close-fitting tunics that ended at the waist or reached to the thigh. But each country and each regiment had its own special tunic, colours and styles. Russian troops wore green; North Germans dark 'Prussian' blue. Swedes wore blue and yellow. Because of their blood-coloured tunics, British troops were nicknamed 'Redcoats'.

Confederate jacket and trousers belonging to a member of the Company K, 20th Georgia Infantry in 1864.

24

Civil defence

As cities grew larger and more densely populated in the 19th century, they needed better protection from natural disasters and crime. Civilian forces, such as police and fire-fighters, were newly founded or reorganised. So that the public would recognise, trust and respect them, they were issued with uniforms in military style.

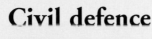

A man from the Thameside Aviation Museum in England models a Victorian fireman's uniform.

Who invented bell-bottom trousers?

American sailors, around 1800.

Uniforms at home

Although new 19th century industries and inventions created jobs - and made profits - there was still a very large gap between rich and poor. Wealthy families could afford to employ large numbers of domestic servants, to cook, clean, care for children, wait at table, run messages, drive horse-drawn carriages and receive visitors to their homes. Male and female servants were expected to be clean, neat and smartly dressed. Employers issued them with uniforms once or twice a year. Servants had to wear the clothes that they were given, however awkward or uncomfortable they were.

A Victorian maid sits down exhausted in Her First Place, by George Dunlop Leslie(1835-1921).

25

WESTERN WORLD 1900 ~ 1950

Most of the years of the early 20th century were scarred by battle. Millions of soldiers, from many nations, died fighting in World War I (1914-1918), and in the revolutions and civil wars that followed. To fill in for the men, millions of women began to work in new careers, outside the home.

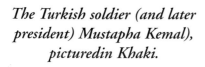

The Turkish soldier (and later president) Mustapha Kemal), picturedin Khaki.

Khaki

Until 1914, many armies still issued bright-coloured uniforms to their men. But improved weapons, such as accurate rifles, and better optical devices, such as binoculars, made these easy to hit at long range. In 1902, British and American armies introduced new, less noticeable uniforms. These were based on greenish-brown clothes worn by late 19th century British troops in India and Africa. Khaki soon became standard issue for armies from Canada and Russia to Japan.

Out to work

Many women were widowed during World War I, and single women were left with little chance of marrying. They all had to go out to work to support themselves. Women found jobs in many different careers. Often, they had to take junior positions, because of male prejudice and their own lack of training. For some jobs, like waiting at table, a uniform was a sign of low rank. For others, like nursing and teaching, it was a proud statement of skilled status.

A waitress serves tea in a London restaurant in 1920.

There was a close link between sports clothes and school uniform. Children's blazers and gym slips were copied from adult sportswear. These hockey players were photographed in 1946 in Wales.

Clothes for school

By around 1900, education was compulsory in many Western nations. In much of Europe, the school uniform was a long-sleeved smock, worn over everyday clothes. But in Britain, uniforms were more elaborate, even for poor pupils. By the 1920s, boys had to wear baggy shorts (usually grey), woollen socks, collared shirts, school ties, caps with badges, and, often, a blazer jacket. Girls also had to wear man-style shirts and ties, knee-length woollen 'gym-slips', blazers and long knitted stockings.

What does the name khaki mean?

It is based on a Hindi (Indian) word meaning 'dust-coloured'.

Battledress, Camouflage, Skirts

In 1939, a second World War was declared. It lasted until 1945. Fighting men, on both sides, wore newly developed uniforms, including camouflage (broken patterns, to help the soldiers hide in fields and woods) and battledress (loose trousers, fastened at the ankle) plus a bloused, long-sleeved top. For the first time, large numbers of women joined the armed forces, and also civilian defence teams. They all wore specially-designed uniforms, based on male styles. However, except for a few specialist tasks, such as motor-maintenance, trousers for women were banned.

Men and women who joined the US aurfirce during World War II wore simple 'forage caps' as part of their uniform.

Late 20th century uniforms were a mixture of traditional and modern. For peaceful tasks or in war, they fulfilled the same needs as earlier uniforms. But they were often made from new, artificial fibres and worn by people doing newly-created jobs.

Chinese Communist Party leader Mao Zedung (1893-1976) wearing a Mao suit, a fashion he imposed on the general Chinese population.

Extreme ideas

Many 20th century wars were fought in difficult terrain -from dense jungle to desert sands. These challenging environments required advanced military clothing. In 1995, the first computer-generated camouflage patterns were pioneered by Canadian scientists. In other nations, old-style uniforms still had a powerful impact. In China, during the Cultural Revolution (1966-1976), troops of Red Guards (young communists) forced the vast Chinese population to wear two-piece 'Mao-suit' uniforms as a sign that they accepted extreme Red Guard policies.

Sport sells

From 1950 onwards, sport was very big business, and sports clothes became a fast-growing part of the international clothing industry. Eye-catching uniforms strengthened a team's brand image, and created profitable opportunities for selling replicas to fans. Streamlined, functional clothes, made of new elastic fibres, helped improve sports performance for professionals and amateurs. Sports-based leisure styles boosted the wearer's morale, by suggesting that they also had an athletes' fitness and fine physique.

American football players wear studded boots, skin-tight, stretchy trousers, and shirts with huge padded shoulders, all in team colours.

Japanese team-workers in a factory in Tokyo, 1995, wearing overalls.

Teamwork

New ways of working, and new products, led to new uniform clothes. In the 1980s and 1990s, Japanese factories pioneered new, team-based, techniques for producing electrical goods and motor vehicles. Team members were loyal to each other, and to the company they worked for. They often wore company uniforms that were light and comfortable to work in, and displayed their team feelings. In other high-tech factories, goods had to be made in dust-free environments. Workers were issued with special uniforms, covering most of the body, including the hair. They were valued for their human skills, hard work and dedication. But, in their uniforms, they looked almost like robots or machines.

Were artificial fibres a good idea for uniforms?

The first artificial fibres were easy to wash, and shed creases. But they could be hot and unhealthy to wear.

Motor services

Changes in society, such as widespread car ownership, created many new jobs, and new demands for uniforms. Motorway police, road accident crew, breakdown service staff and traffic wardens all wore distinctive clothes. These identified them as they patrolled the streets, and increased their authority when dealing with people who might be injured, shocked or hostile.

A UK traffic warden. He is dressed in a uniform very similar to a British police officer's.

29

GLOBAL STYLES TODAY

Today, just as thousands of years ago, uniforms are used to create a sense of belonging. Technology has resulted in ever more sophisticated uniforms, yet, traditional dress codes are making a new impact, and trendy shoppers are creating their own 'uniforms' by purchasing clothes that look like those of all the other people in their chosen group.

Better performance

Designers of military uniforms aim to make clothes that will perform well under pressure. Most new uniforms, such as the US Army Combat Uniform (ACU) featured loose shirts worn over wide trousers. Garments are made of mixed green, grey and tan camouflage cloth. They have Velcro (R) tabs to fasten badges showing the wearer's name, rank and duties, and built-in **infra-red** squares allowing wearers to be identified in the dark.

A US officer poses with the Interceptor body armor small-arms protective inserts.

Riot Gear

Under fire, soldiers, police and security guards put on body armour. This protects them, hides their individual identity, and helps them appear as part of a formidable team. It makes use of ancient designs such as the metal flap (or ridge) at the back of the neck first seen on Roman helmets. But it also features modern manufactured materials, such as transparent plastic and shock absorbing foam.

A US soldier shown wearing the latest Army Combat Uniform (ACU) in 2005.

Religion and politics

Today, as in the past, clothes can make a religious or political statement. For example, governments and religious leaders in some Muslim countries encourage male and female citizens to put on hijab (modest dress). To them, Muslim 'uniform' styles, such as the all-covering abayah (cloak), are a positive way for Muslims to proclaim their faith. They can also be methods of enforcing religious or political conformity.

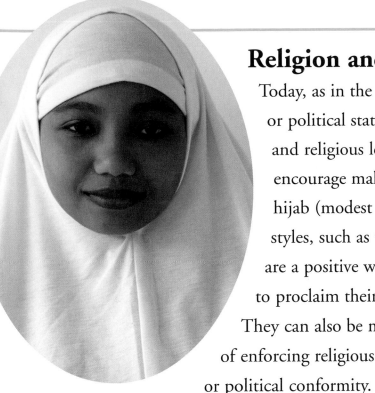

The Muslim khimar (headscarf), which is part of the hijab

What do US serving personnel wear under their ACU?

Moisture-wicking t-shirt, underwear and socks, made from high-tech artificial fibre.

Worldwide style

Today's media mean that news about clothes and fashions can spread quickly all round the world. Different social groups choose their own styles of clothing. These 'uniforms' are made to seem more attractive to wearers by pressure from their peers (equals), and by marketing campaigns. Uniforms today are less compulsory and class-driven, and more a way for the wearer to announce to the world characteristics they want to identify with.

Today, when Western people have more time, freedom and money to choose clothing than ever before, many still like to wear a uniform, such as jeans and t-shirt, or baseball caps and hoodies.

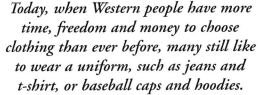

berserkers Viking warriors who wore bearskin shirts and fought furiously.

buckskin Deerskin.

caliphs Muslim rulers who led the Sunni (majority) Muslim community.

candidates People who run for election to public office.

cataracts Waterfalls on the River Nile in Egypt, North Africa.

cavalary Soldiers who fight on horseback.

chain mail Body protection made from linked metal rings.

city state A city that rules itself and the land around it.

crook Hooked stick.

drama Plays and acting. Originally, the acting out of myths and legends in Ancient Greece.

epaulettes Shoulder decorations.

flail Heavy rod.

habits Plain, sober clothes worn by monks, nuns and friars.

hoplites Citizen foot-soldiers in Ancient Greece.

infra-red Rays of energy given out by hot objects, including the Sun. They cannot be seen but can be felt.

Mesopotamia Land between the River Tigris and the River Euphrates, in the Middle East. Now part of Iraq.

murmillo Gladiator in Ancient Rome equipped with a heavy helmet and shield.

nemes Egyptian head-covering made of cloth.

piety Respect for the gods.

plate armour Body protection made of carefully-shaped pieces of metal.

repentance Being sorry for sins.

retarius Gladiator in Ancient Rome who fought using a net and a trident.

rosettes Circular decorations made of ribbon or braid.

saffron A deep yellow dye made from crocus-flowers.

secutor Gladiator in Ancient Rome equipped with tough leather armour.

senators Members of the ruling council in Ancient Rome.

shaman Magic healer.

surcoat Loose cloth robe worn on top of armour.

sufism A Muslim spiritual movement. Members meditate (think deeply) and sometimes dance to try to communicate with God.

talisman Lucky charm; object believed to have magic powers.

terracotta Baked clay.

trident Three-pronged spear.